Father John's Story

by Sara Shea

Cover photo provided by Mrs. Bozena Rosicka, Czech Republic

Back cover photo © the McCook Daily Gazette in Nebraska

ISBN 978-0-615-61192-1

Published in 2012 by Sara E. Shea. Printed by Lulu.com.

© 2012 Sara E. Shea. All rights reserved.

"Did you ever pray for anything
that you knew was never going to happen,
but you kept on praying for it anyway?

Well that is exactly what I did, I prayed every
day for forty years about going back.
And it finally happened."

Rev. John Prachar

Introduction

Every life has a story to tell. We can find pieces of stories in conversations, letters, journals, obituaries, church records, family trees, even Facebook pages. If you are famous, someone will probably interview you at length, take pictures of you, follow you around, question your friends and family, and write your biography for all to read.

But what if you're not famous?

And what if you lived your last forty years in quiet, small-town America, before the internet, and then you died unexpectedly, without leaving behind any journals or spouse or children?

Well, that would be a difficult story to tell. I am compelled to try, however, because I believe I know one worth preserving. It is a story I have known my whole life, a story about forty years of quiet living and waiting, but it is also a story of history and war and refugees and Nazis and communists. It is about persecution of the Catholic clergy and prayer and survival and hope and healing. It is about Nebraska and immigration and homelands and freedom.

It is the story of Father John Prachar, a Czech priest who became an American citizen and devoted most of his life to serving the people of southern Nebraska. His photo is in my baby book, because he is the priest who baptized me as an infant. Before he died, in 1991, a few local newspapers interviewed him about his life, providing me with the basis for many of my facts and all of my quotations. I also have the information stored in the archives of the Diocese of Lincoln, a few letters from people who knew him, and bits and pieces from researching in books and online.

I know that popular media these days likes to tell us about the absolute worst priests in existence. I have personally known dozens of Catholic priests well during my life, however, and all of their life stories are good ones worth sharing. They are just men with very simple life missions, to "preach the Gospel of Christ at all times, using words as necessary," so the saying goes. Father John was like that, too. He didn't spend his time writing down his thoughts and memories, but I wish he had. Then, you could read his words instead of mine. You'll have to blame him for that.

Shortly before he died, Father John said of his life, "This is a story of joy, extreme joy."

Here is that story.

Who was John Prachar? To start to answer that, we must also ask what was Czechoslovakia, for the life of John and the life of that nation were indelibly intertwined. Both were born in 1918 and died in 1991. In 1992, Czechoslovakia began making peaceful arrangements to divide into two countries, Slovakia and the Czech Republic, which is how we know of them today.

John was born first of the two, on April 8th, 1918, in a little village called Dlouha Lhota in the district of Tabor, south of Prague. He had two brothers (one named Frank) and two sisters (Marie Janu and Anna Penka.) As an infant he was brought by his parents to St. Wenceslaus Catholic Church in the nearby town of Choustnik to be baptized. St. Wenceslaus, who was killed in the year 929, is the patron saint of the Czech Republic, and many Catholic churches throughout the world have been named in his honor.

Just six months after John was born, in October of 1918, the Czech and Slovak people received their independence from the Austro-Hungarian Empire which had just been defeated in the First World War. This long-desired independence allowed them to birth a new country together, Czechoslovakia, and establish a democracy with a constitution based on the constitution of the United States. "We used the good part and corrected all the errors," John would later say jokingly. At that time, Czechoslovakia was ranked among the top ten wealthiest nations in the world. The Czech culture had existed in the same areas of Europe for *more than a thousand years.* The twentieth century would prove to be very, very hard on this ancient people.

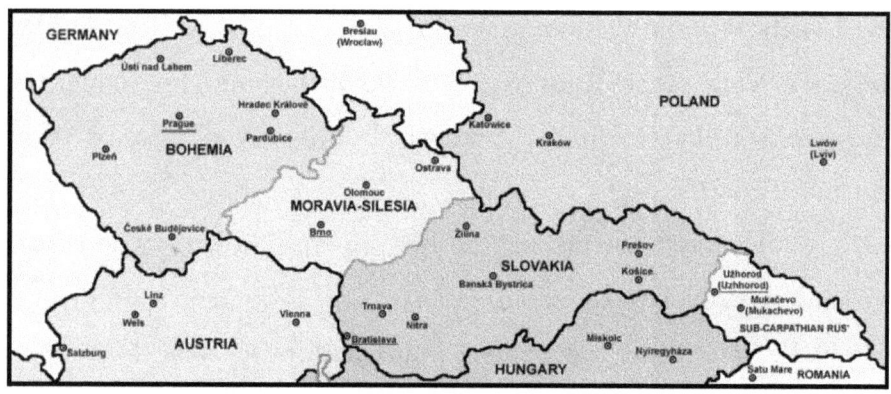

Public domain image.

In 1918, Czechoslovakia seemed like a wonderful place to live. It seemed like a fine place to raise children, help them grow, and watch them craft their lives. Unfortunately for millions of people, however,

November of that same year was when a young soldier in neighboring Germany became filled with insane rage at the leadership of his own country as they surrendered, ending their fighting in the First World War. That young soldier, an orphan, a high-school drop-out, a one-time homeless man who sold water-paintings on the street - his name was Adolf Hitler. His irrational rage would focus his ambitions. And soon enough, this man's decisions would disrupt the intended life of John Prachar and countless others forever.

But not yet. John first spent his happy, innocent years of early childhood in the family home, and then from the ages of six to twelve he attended the grade school in Choustnik. His family attended Sunday Mass at St. Wenceslaus, where John also received first Holy Communion and Confirmation. Although the Prachar's spoke Czech at home, John also learned to speak the Slovak language during these years at school.

The age of 13 brought a major change to John's life. Because he had done well in elementary school, his family wanted him to continue his studies at "gymnasium," which was an eight-year program of study combining both high school and college curricula. The nearest gymnasium was a boarding school in the southern city of Ceske Budejovice (formerly called Budweis, a city famous for its beer.) Here John lived and studied, supported by his parents, until he was 21. The name of the school was Ceskeslovenske Statni Gymnsium Jirsikove.

Despite living in a predominately Catholic country, some of John's school teachers happened to be atheist. One of them in particular, a biology teacher, challenged many of the religious ideas that John's parents had taught him. From the earliest age he could remember, John had been intrigued by the Catholic priesthood and wondered about being a priest, but in school he began to wonder if "God" as he knew Him even existed. Had all Jews and Christians been deceived into believing something completely untrue? John couldn't figure out what he believed for sure and he questioned everything.

In January of 1933, while John was 15 and in gymnasium, Hitler became Chancellor of next-door Germany and began working in earnest towards his goals of conquering the world and destroying everyone who did not agree with him or look like him. As unbelievable as it sounds, by taking things one step at a time, by getting like-minded and morally weak people to help him, and by deceiving people all along the way, his horrific plan was actually set into motion.

When John was 20, in September of 1938, at a meeting in Munich, Hitler persuaded Great Britain (through Neville Chamberlain) and France (through Edouard Daladier) to allow him to take an area called the Sudetenland away from Czechoslovakia. No one from Czechoslovakia was invited to this meeting. The Sudetenland was mostly populated by German-speaking people anyway, Hitler argued.

In return, he promised to not take land away from any other European nations. This so-called Munich Agreement was despised and feared by Czechoslovakia, of course, and many other world leaders, but Chamberlain and Daladier hoped it would prevent the start of a war with Germany. They were wrong.

Czechoslovakia prior to World War II, with the Sudetenland colored in black. Public domain image.

The Sudetenland, a region of some 11,000 square miles, was a strategic piece of land because it contained highly fortified mountains and forests and would have been difficult for the German army to take by force from the excellent Czech army. On October 1st, immediately after the Munich Agreement was announced, Germany occupied the region. Hitler had no intentions of stopping there. He waited for winter to pass, and then on March 15th, 1939, his army easily attacked and conquered the entire country of Czechoslovakia. John was almost 21 years old and was just getting ready to graduate. Military rule was established. The world was shocked.

Two days later, the *Manchester Guardian*, a Czech newspaper, posted the following:

> Prague, a sorrowing Prague, yesterday had its first day of German rule - a day in which the Czechs learned of the details of their subjection to Germany, and in which the Germans began their measures against the Jews and against those people who have "opened their mouths too wide."
>
> Prague's streets were jammed with silent pedestrians wandering about, looking out of the corners of their eyes at German soldiers carrying guns, at armoured cars, and at other military precautions. Some Czechs were seen turning up their noses at the Germans. Germans were everywhere. Bridges were occupied by troops and each bridge-head had a heavy machine-gun mounted on a tripod and pointing to the sky. Every twenty yards along the pavement two

machine-guns were mounted facing each other.

Suicides have begun. The fears of the Jews grow. The funds of the Jewish community have been seized, stopping Jewish relief work. The Prague Bar Council has ordered all its "non-Aryan" members [lawyers] to stop practicing at once. The organization for Jewish emigration has been closed. Hundreds of people stood outside the British Consulate shouting: "We want to get away!"

This is only the beginning. According to an official spokesman of the German Foreign Office in Berlin last night, the Gestapo (secret police) will have rounded up hundreds of "harmful characters" within the next few days. So far about fifty to a hundred men have been put in local gaols. "There are certain centres of resistance which need to be cleaned up," said the spokesman. "Also some people open their mouths too wide. Some of them neglected to get out in time. They may total several thousand before we are through. Remember that Prague was a breeding-place for opposition to National Socialism."

The head of the Gestapo in Prague is reported to have been more definite: "We have 10,000 arrests to carry out." Already, say Reuter's correspondent, everyone seems to have an acquaintance who has disappeared…

Beginning immediately, and continuing for the next six years, thousands of Czechoslovakians protested the German occupation. One night, some Allied Czech soldiers even parachuted into the country and killed one of the major Nazi leaders. Nearly all of the resistance groups were led by college students. Yet nothing they tried to do seemed to make any difference. The Nazis always responded to dissent swiftly and powerfully, sometimes destroying entire villages as retribution. Every monastery and convent was closed. As early as 1939 they started closing the universities in Czechoslovakia and sent as many as 1200 students to prison or to work camps. Some student leaders were even murdered.

Czechoslovakia was also home to large resources of uranium, prompting Albert Einstein to caution President Roosevelt in a letter during August of 1939:

> I understand that Germany has actually stopped the sale of uranium from the Czechoslovakian mines which she has taken over. That she should have taken such early action might perhaps be understood on the ground that the son of the German Under-Secretary of State, von Weizsicker, is attached to the Kaiser-Wilhelm-Institut in Berlin where some of the American

work on uranium is now being repeated...

In the midst of all this, John graduated from gymnasium and seriously debated which path to follow next. Should he join the resistance? Should he move back home, or train for a career which would support a wife and family? Should he consider working for the Church? He had done well in school, and his uncle offered to finance his way through a medical school. But John still had a lot of unanswered questions about life. There was an unrelenting desire in his soul to study philosophy and theology, and to have some time to ask questions and pursue their true answers.

Believers consider such desires to be whisperings of the Holy Spirit. Prudently, John didn't dismiss them. He decided he would enter the seminary in his diocese. He would study the big questions of life, and decide who he thought was right, his biology teacher or his parents and the church?

So, in 1939, despite the German occupation, John began his studies at Saint Anna's Seminary in the same town where he graduated from gymnasium, Ceske Budejovice. He studied Sacred Scripture, history, theology, and a lot of philosophy. He went to Mass every day. He began to daily pray the Liturgy of the Hours which is prayed by all priests and many religious and lay people. These prayers, contained in the Breviary, include prayers for specific times such as morning prayer and evening prayer. Also included are the Psalms and other Scriptures, hymns, prayers for the world, and spiritual writings. John did everything that his Bishop asked of him.

    These years of formation would test and teach him. Gradually, over the next three years, John grew to believe in God more and more, and to love the idea of being a priest and serving the Church for the rest of his life. This desire is a necessary part of discerning any vocation. The fact that Western Catholic priests also take a vow of celibacy, in imitation of Christ, is obviously an additional factor in priestly discernment. John saw this vow as an opportunity to dedicate himself undividedly, 24 hours a day, to his ministry. Forgoing the joys of marriage would be a sacrifice, but it was one that John was beginning to think, with the help of God, that he could make.

Most seminarians throughout Church history have spent their years of formation studying, doing light volunteer work, praying quietly, and enjoying fellowship with other Christian men and women. John's formation, however, would soon include a lengthy and horribly unjust trial of body and soul.

It was 1941 and in the midst of his studies, what would be called World War II was moving into full swing all around him in Europe. By the end of the year, the United States would also be pulled into the war by the Japanese attack on Pearl Harbor on December 7th.

From Germany, Hitler had a huge war to fight, and he needed equipment. In many countries, the economy will benefit from wartime government spending, but Hitler wouldn't ever consider paying Jews or Christians for their work. He ordered "labor camps" to be built. One of these was would be called Grenzweg [or Grenzwek, or Grenznea] by the prisoners; it was near Koethen [or Anhalt], Germany, just south of Berlin. It was adjacent to an airplane factory, and laborers were needed.

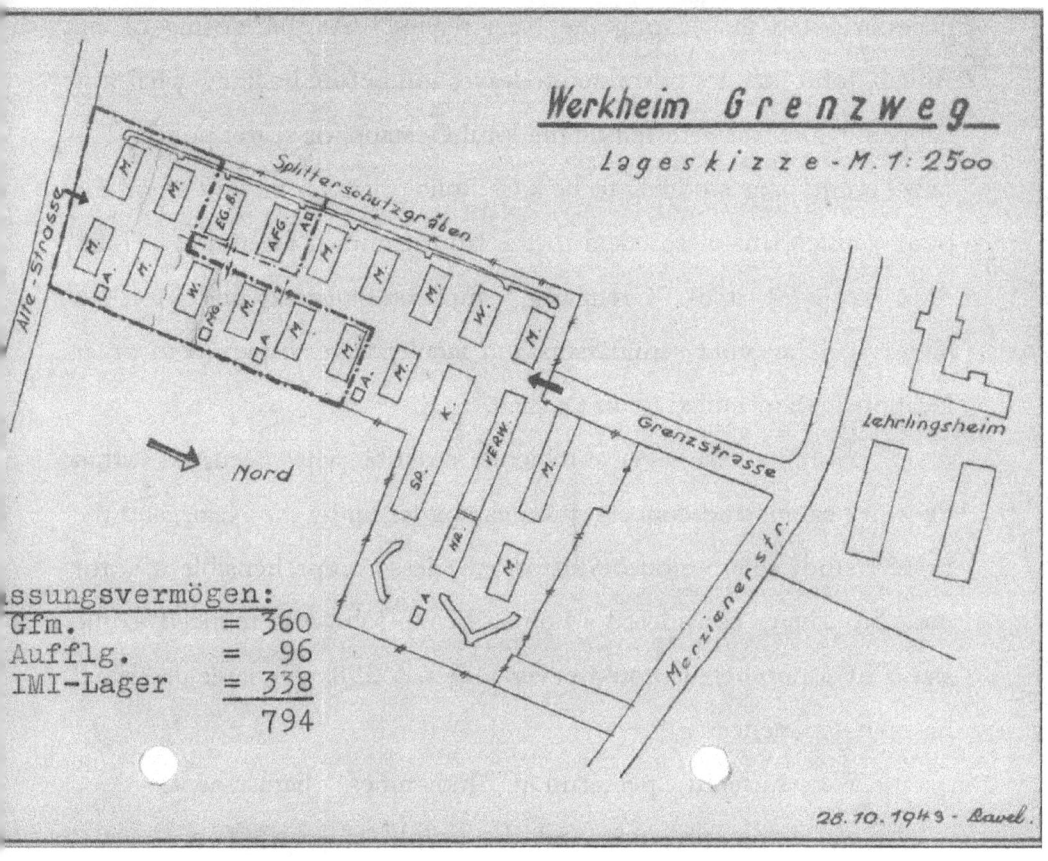

This is a 1943 drawing of the Grenzweg labor camp on the eastern side of Kothen, Germany

The following year, 1942, during John's fourth year of theology, before he was ordained a deacon and without warning, the seminary where he lived and studied was closed by the government. Martin Bormann, who was eventually second-in-command to Hitler, had launched an internal war against the Christian churches. He wrote that year that their power "must absolutely and finally be broken" as a necessary step in securing the Nazi regime. At the closing of St. Anna's, John was not permitted to leave, and before he knew what was happening, he was arrested by the local Gestapo, or secret police. His only "crime" was studying to be a Catholic priest. John and 10 of the other seminarians were taken to the labor camp in Grenzweg. (John once wrote of it as "Grenzweg - Junkers Flugzeug und Motoren Werke.") The other seminarians and faculty were dispersed to other locations. Many ended up in Dachau.

Words could never sufficiently describe what occurred within the work camps and concentration camps set up by the Nazis, and the more I study this period of history, the less comprehensible it is for me. No longer considered a human being, John was reduced to the status of a number he could never forget: 59298. He later described his own experience:

> We suffered persecution, indignities, harassment, starvation, privation and the untold anguish of not knowing whether our loved ones were dead or alive....
> We worked 12 hours a day, or night, depending upon the shift. We had one meal in 24 hours, which consisted of a few potatoes and gravy or soup - a few vegetables swimming in water. We received a piece of bread every other day...

The prisoners were given just enough food and medical

treatment to be kept alive and working. John would remember the constant thirst and hunger pain, the constant threat of being shot if he disobeyed an order, and the inhumane living quarters. He was often bored by the monotony, he missed his family and friends, especially during the holidays, and his soul longed deeply for the Sacraments. His specific task at the factory was working on a machine grinding teeth for the very heavy wheels of airplanes. To say the least, it was not the type of work he was accustomed to doing all day.

Each morning, John woke up in Grenzweg wondering if it would be the day of his death. Some of the men, crazed by their maltreatment, especially their hunger, would eventually speak their minds, erupt at a guard, or refuse to obey a command. At this camp, prisoners would instantly be shot for this behavior. John wondered how long he could continue before he would reach his own breaking point. In the early months, he was filled with anger towards the Nazi guards for their brutality and heartlessness.

The prisoners all assumed that the guards would kill them if any of the Allied troops approached the camp, and that only a miracle could save them from their situation. Death loomed always immanent. Many years later, John remembered the bleak outlook that the prisoners had. He said, "We knew if Hitler won, we would be there until we died. And if he lost, he would kill us so there wouldn't be any witnesses. There was no hope [of survival]." Indeed, in many of the camps, evidence was destroyed and prisoners were executed or sent on "death marches" to nowhere when Allied troops got near.

Yet it was here, under these circumstances, that John first began to really talk to God. He could have given in to the temptation to despair, to believe that even God couldn't save him, but he didn't. John entrusted himself continually to the mercy of God. He often contemplated the death of his savior, Christ Jesus. He thought about how unjust and painful Christ's crucifixion had been. Christ had been so alone up on that cross. And yet, John remembered, Christ's mother was near to Him to the end, even though Jesus couldn't always see her. Like St. Maximillian Kolbe and St. Teresa Benedicta of the Cross (Edith Stein,) who both died in Nazi concentration camps, John believed in the powerful, healing intercession of the Blessed Virgin Mary.

John knew that Christ had suffered to open the gates of Heaven Eternal. Each day this belief alone gave John the hope to keep living for just one more day. His sufferings could be united to those of Jesus on the cross, and thus be used to help himself and others. The American philosopher Peter Kreeft has written it this way: "And [Jesus] shows us that we can henceforth use our very brokenness as nourishment for those we love. Since we are His body, we too are the bread that is broken for others." Of his own body broken down, John would later simply say, "I learned to believe in prayer. At times it looked impossible, but I continued to pray."

Even in the face of certain death, the human spirit can

struggle to survive. John found that the bond of captivity he shared with the other prisoners was an unexpected source of strength, saying:

> If I ever lived through a period of love, it was in the labor camp. We never asked what religion a man had. Whether you're Catholic or Protestant, when you're starving or sick it hurts the same way. Conditions were terrible and the weaker men died under the strain. Once when I was very sick, a fellow prisoner secretly gave me a raw egg to eat which helped me greatly. I knew that he had stolen it and would be shot if caught. He was Lutheran, yet he took that risk to save me. We lived in love.

So for three years, from 1942-1945, John suffered. He worked. He prayed. And he smoked as many cigarettes as he could get. This little "luxury" was the only one that his captors didn't prevent within the camp. John would later say, "it helped to kill the pain of being hungry." Nicotine, like alcohol, is addictive, but both substances have their legitimate places in this world. John could worry about addictions later if he survived.

In early 1945 rumors began leaking into the camp that Allied forces were getting closer. The guards did their best to deny them, but everyone could feel that tensions were starting to run high. John always felt thoroughly angry about being forced to build airplanes for the enemy, and as the hopes of an Allied advancement became more real, he recalled, "We prayed to be bombed because we were all Hitler's enemies and we knew the factory was important to the Nazi war effort. Eventually, we were bombed and many of the men died."

The bombing occurred in the morning hours of early May, 1945, awaking John from sleep. At first, fear ran through him. The walls were shaking, and some of the men were screaming in pain. Then John and the others suddenly realized that something was different in the camp... there weren't any guards outside of the barracks! They had all fled during the night. This was a huge, unexpected surprise to everyone. So the prisoners ran outside and saw standing right in front of them what they had been longing so intensely for: the tanks and soldiers of the United States Army. They were under the command of General George S. Patton.

The prisoners learned that the camp at Dachau had just been liberated on April 30th, and May 8th was deemed VE Day - Victory in Europe Day. The following day, it was announced that the more than three million American troops in Europe would soon be heading home or moved on to the Pacific Theater.

John remembered his liberation clearly: "One day my prayers were answered and the guards were gone. One of the most beautiful sights I have ever seen was when I saw the colors of the United States flag and knew that the American troops had liberated Germany... As did many other prisoners I wept with joy and thanksgiving for that awe-inspiring country, America, and for her sons who had come across an ocean to die for us so that we might be free."

The first freedom John enjoyed was the freedom to leave the camp. He weighed less than a hundred pounds now, after entering the camp weighing a hundred and fifty. The Americans fed the prisoners what they could. In a daze, John set out on foot. Where should he go? The nearest person he knew could help him was a priest who lived a hundred miles away in Czechoslovakia. So for a week he walked in that direction and kept walking until he got there. All along the way he met other people who were displaced by the war. He heard horrific tales about the concentration camps and other labor camps. Some of the villages he saw had been reduced to rubble.

John was eventually home again. The war was over.

John liked to sum up his years at Grenzweg by simply saying, "I learned to believe in prayer." Back home in Czechoslovakia, John was gradually reunited with his parents and family members and friends, with old classmates and professors. Others were missing or dead. Wenceslaus Sladky, John's former seminary roommate, didn't recognize John anymore because he had lost a third of his weight. (Sladky was later ordained and moved to the United States.)

It would be years before the full extent of the Nazi carnage was realized. It is thought that at least eleven million people lost their lives to Hitler. Some estimates even approach twelve million. Within these, over a million victims were children, six million were Jewish, and six million were Polish. Of the Poles, at least half were Christian, nearly all of whom were Catholic. Of all Europe, Poland was the hardest-hit country; one in six Poles perished during the war. Eighteen percent of their clergy were annihilated.

In John's native Czechoslovakia, 300,000 citizens had lost their lives during the war. John learned that 109 Catholic priests from his homeland had been taken to the Dachau concentration camp in Germany, where 2579 Catholic priests were imprisoned together in separate barracks, surrounded by double layers of barbed-wire fence, to prevent them from ministering to the other prisoners in the camp.

Everyone John talked to had a heart-wrenching story to tell.

As knowledge of the war and the Holocaust spread, sadness filled the country and the world. John had survived, but millions had not. This realization frequently brought him to his knees in thanksgiving, but also in contemplation. "Why, Lord?" everyone kept asking, and John was no exception.

It was so hard to resume "normal life" after the war. Fathers, mothers, children were all missing. Everyone was mourning. And the country's troubles were far from over, even now. After six years of occupation by Germany, the Allied Powers now permitted Russia to oversee post-war Czechoslovakia. Over the course of just three years, a communist government with total control was established, and Joseph Stalin, the Soviet Premier in Russia, greatly influenced the new leaders of the country.

John later remembered thinking, "First Hitler and then Stalin. Was there to be no end to the persecution? No freedom to love God and man? No place or circumstance to call 'home'?"

In theory, communism means that everyone is treated equally, and all material goods are divided equally. The very first Christian communities lived somewhat like this. They were small in number, however, and ruled by the many ideals of the Gospel. Theirs was a freely chosen lifestyle. In contrast, throughout history, communism has been forced upon large groups of people, as it was in Czechoslovakia in the 1940's, and in every case it has failed to provide a just system of governance. By controlling all infrastructure and industry, without the "checks and balances" of a judiciary or of representation, then the power becomes centralized and is easily corrupted. In essence, communism has always ended up a dictatorship. Because the citizens all receive the same payment for their jobs, regardless of how hard they work, many of the best and brightest workers become frustrated and disillusioned.

In Czechoslovakia, the communist leaders were atheist. They permitted the Churches to stay open, to keep rebellions from happening, but they began threatening any priest who preached against the government, as Hitler had done just a decade earlier.

Despite knowing this was the situation, John continued to feel a calling to the priesthood. Pope Benedict the Sixteenth once discussed this intuition of being called to the priesthood when he spoke to a group of seminarians saying:

> The seminarian experiences the beauty of that call in a moment of grace which could be defined as 'falling in love.' His soul is filled with amazement, which makes

him ask in prayer: 'Lord, why me?' But love knows no 'why'; it is a free gift to which one responds with the gift of self... You have not chosen Him; He has chosen you. Here is the secret of your vocation and your mission.[1]

Believing indeed that Christ had chosen him, John decided to resume his formal seminary studies in Ceske Budejovice. He was still surrounded by mourning and suffering, but he knew that much of life was mystery, and that suffering was the biggest mystery of all.

Mystery implies that there is no possibility of reaching full understanding. For believers, God Himself is a mystery, beyond comprehension, for He is infinite and we are finite. Saint Paul spoke of this when he wrote, "For now we see in a mirror dimly, but then [in Heaven] face to face. Now I know in part; then I shall understand fully, even as I have been fully understood." (1 Cor. 13:12) God gives us our intellects so that we can think through life rationally, and He additionally *reveals* to us all that we need to know that is beyond the limit of mere reason. Two things that the Catholic Church teaches about suffering are that we are never alone in our suffering, for Christ is always with us, and that all suffering can be redemptive, for ourselves or for others, when it is united to the sufferings of Christ. Another survivor of the Holocaust, a woman from Holland named

---

1 August 19, 2005, in Cologne, Germany during World Youth Day.

Corrie ten Boom, beautifully described the mystery of suffering this way: "No matter how deep our darkness, He is deeper still."

John knew that as a priest he might not always be able to give people all of the answers they wanted, but he knew that he would be able to give them Jesus. He took comfort in this Gospel story he liked to quote later in life:

> Jesus looked at [the apostles] and said, "With men [salvation] is impossible, but not with God; for all things are possible with God." Peter began to say to him, "Lo, we have left everything and followed you." Jesus said, "Truly, I say to you, there is no one who has left house or brothers or sisters or mother or father or children or lands, for my sake and for the gospel, who will not receive a hundredfold now in this time, houses and brothers and sisters and mothers and children and lands, with persecutions, and in the age to come eternal life." (Mark 10:27-30)

And so on July 7th, 1946, at the age of 28, with certitude in his heart and mind, John Prachar answered Christ's invitation to the priesthood. He received the Sacrament of Holy Orders in the Cathedral of St. Nicholas in Ceske Budejovice. He was ordained by the Most Reverend Anton Eltschkner, Auxiliary Bishop of Prague. Father John later recalled: "After all the misery and cruelty that I had seen, I thought Christ was the only answer, so I decided to finish my studies and become a priest under the communist regime. My friends thought I was nuts. They suggested that I was going to end up in Siberia." Then responding in his typical, light-hearted manner, Father John would say: "Well, I like to travel!"

Holy Orders is received when a Bishop recites the prayers of ordination and lays his hands on the head of the recipient, continuing through time a physical link all the way back to the Apostles. This Sacrament, which was instituted by Christ at the Last Supper, empowers the man to say Mass, forgive sins, confirm, anoint, and preach the faith. Every priest remains under the obedience of his local bishop for as long as he lives. Father John knew that it was through this obedience that God would continually reveal to him His divine will, and this knowledge brought him great comfort and peace. After his ordination, he went to his home town of Choustnik to offer his first Holy Mass at St. Wenceslaus Church. Attended by all of his family and friends who were able, the event was a time of great joy.

Fr. John's first assignment as a new priest was a brief stay as an assistant in the town of Veseli nad Luznici. This was followed by his first pastorship, to the village of Cerna, in southern Czechoslovakia, at the Church of the Immaculate Conception of the Virgin Mary. Here he also had two small mission parishes, in Polna and Dolni Vltavice. Little did he know when he moved into the rectory of Cerna that these would be the *last* parishes he would ever get to serve in his home country.

This photo of Father John was taken while he was serving in Cerna and provided by parishioner Mrs. Bozena Rosicka.

Each day in Cerna Father John awoke and spent time preparing for Mass. As a new priest, this was his greatest joy and highest privilege. Many sanctuaries have this little reminder written somewhere: "Dear priest of God, say this Mass as if it were your first Mass, your last Mass, and your only Mass." Father John, in his early fervor, always tried to follow this good reminder. He would carefully read and study the biblical passages before each Mass and prepare a homily about them. Preaching is a key part of the parish priest's duties. After surviving the Second World War and being immersed in the injustices of communism, the parishioners of Cerna were in great need of Christ's comforting message, and Father John did his best to speak to them of God's loving concern.

After Mass, Father John would visit with his parishioners and get to know them. He shared meals with them, and blessed their homes. One family in particular, the Rosicka's, quickly befriended the young priest and often invited him into their home. Mrs. Bozena Rosicka later described Father John as "a dear man… made of gold. He never caused anyone harm, he was always helping where needed, and he behaved like a true patriot… He was cheerful." She recalled him being very frugal, and preferring simple meals such as potatoes with milk.

Father John also befriended the Tomandl and Lovetinsky families, among others. When dining alone, he would take his meals at the local inn, called *U Tomandlu*. He would visit the sick of the community and anoint them, teach religion classes, counsel people, prepare couples for marriage and witness their vows during their weddings. He would baptize the new babies, and frequently he would hear the confessions of his parishioners. In the wintertime, he would shovel snow away from the churches, and each spring he would organize the planting of flowers around the statues in the gardens.

Cerna is alongside a large lake, Lake Lipno, where there are fishing, boating and ice skating opportunities. It is also surrounded by beautiful paths for hiking or biking or skiing. There were community dances every weekend, and Father John would join in this fun, but Mrs. Rosicka recalls him always leaving "before it got too late." In addition to these occasional recreations, Father John continued to pray his Breviary throughout the day, and he would study the Scriptures and spend time praying quietly.

This was the life that young John envisioned when he first began his seminary studies, but things were about to drastically change for him. Again.

Father John spent nearly three years in Cerna. This entire time Czechoslovakia continued under a Communist rule which was constantly growing in power. Thousands of citizens, including numerous priests, were unjustly arrested under the suspicion of opposing the government, and many were never seen from again. Nothing could be spoken or written that would suggest that things weren't right or could be better. Very quickly, as had happened under

Nazi occupation, the priests were pressured to quit preaching about the Scriptures and instead to speak about the benefits of communism. The government wanted the priests to help boost the morale of the citizens.

It was 1949. The vast majority of priests were refusing to cooperate with these communist "suggestions." Father John's own bishop, the Very Rev. Joseph Hlouch, had been arrested and sent to an unknown prison earlier in the year. Every bishop in Czechoslovakia would eventually face house arrest or imprisonment - some for decades - if they were unwilling to support and obey the communist leaders. Father John would later recall: "They were arresting one priest after another. The parishioners that I served in Cerna were beautiful people. They would come to Mass and say that the government was arresting priests and they worried about me. *I would tell them that somebody had to tell the truth.*" He identified with the prophet Jeremiah, who tried to stifle his own tongue from speaking the truth: "If I say, 'I will not mention Him, or speak any more in His name,' there is in my heart as it were a burning fire shut up in my bones, and I am weary with holding it in, and I cannot." (Jeremiah 20:9)

The secret police in Czechoslovakia at the time was called the STB (Statni Tajna Bezpecnost.) It resembled the Russian KGB. In many towns, including Cerna, local communist supporters joined the STB as informants. Two informants in Cerna were assigned to keep an eye on Father John. They would take turns sitting at the back of the Church during Mass to listen to what was being preached. They also soon discovered that Father John was part of an informal network offering shelter to the many people who were trying to flee across the Czech border. These travelers would walk up to Father John and use the passwords, "overnight at the rectory, please," and without another word, Father would escort them to his rectory for a safe place to sleep for the night.

Despite wanting to speak boldly against the communists, Father John's parishioners reminded him that if he did so, then he certainly would be arrested and most likely murdered. They tried to convince him to leave the country and return to them, alive, once the government was overthrown. For several months he felt tormented and kept praying about what he should do.

Father John thought about his mission as a priest, which was to help spread the Gospel "to the ends of the world." He was Czech by nationality, he spoke the Czech language, and he loved the Czech people. But perhaps, through the voices of his parishioners, God was trying to tell him that he should try to stay alive and serve Him somewhere else, at least for a little while. He was still plagued by memories of his recent years in the labor camp. He would later say, "I did not feel I was physically strong enough to go through the prison experience again. Had I truly wanted to be a hero, I would have gone, but I felt there had to be a more effective way to fight communism."

So, he decided he would leave. First, he needed a plan. He

wanted to visit his family - especially his parents - to say goodbye. He needed transportation, money, a destination. He needed time. But all of this was not to be.

On Saturday, April 8th, 1949, Father John celebrated his 31st birthday. The following day was Palm Sunday, when the Church recalls the prophesied entrance of Jesus into Jerusalem the week before He died, and the start of Holy Week, the most special week of the year. Four days later, on April 13th, was Holy Thursday. This is the night when the Church remembers the Last Supper of Christ, the night before His crucifixion. It was on this night that Jesus celebrated the annual Jewish Passover feast with his twelve apostles.

During the several hours that these men spent together, Jesus taught them extensively. He washed their feet, told them that He was going to build a home for them in heaven, "so that where I am you also may be." And most importantly, Jesus lifted up the symbolic bread and wine of the feast and told His apostles that they were His body and blood, and that they were to repeat this meal in His memory.

Now that's a holy order! Christ had ordained these men to be His priests.

Father John celebrated the Holy Thursday liturgy with great joy, knowing that his calling as a priest was the very same calling received by the apostles. As soon as the Mass was over, however, as he was turning off the lights and locking up the building, a policeman stepped inside to give him an urgent message. Risking his own life, this man - whose identity was never revealed - told Father John that he needed to leave the country that very night. Tomorrow, he had found out, the STB intended to arrest him.

"Father, you must run. There is no time left."

Without further details, the man hurriedly left the church, not wanting anyone to know that he had been there. Father John's heart began to pound. He wasn't prepared to leave so soon, but he knew that he must go right away. "I was told if I wanted to save my life, I should leave. They were planning to arrest me." The first thing he did was to approach the tabernacle, remove the sacred host, and consume it. The Eucharist deserves protection from those who would desecrate it, and Father knew that he couldn't trust the local police to protect the church building in his absence. He went outside and around to the front of the church and locked the door, dropping the church key into his coat pocket. Walking away for the last time, he glanced up at the high steeple and told himself that he would be back to see it again some day.

Back in his rectory, Father John changed out of his clerics and put on civilian clothing. He wore "riding pants and high boots" since his only mode of transportation was his motorcycle. He put his coat back on, and his hat. What should he take with him? He grabbed what cash and cigarettes he had in the rectory, shoved them into his pockets, and looked around him at his home. He opened a drawer and took out a flashlight, added that to his coat pocket. Wondering what to do next, he fell to his knees for a moment, covering his face with his hands, begging the Lord to guide him.

Thoughts of Saint Joseph and the Blessed Virgin filled his mind, reminding him of the night that angels awoke St. Joseph and told him to flee with his family immediately to Egypt. Jesus was only an infant then, which made their whole journey much more difficult and complicated. Father had only himself to look after. This thought gave him courage.

Father John left the rectory and went outside. Standing in the driveway, he quickly debated which direction he should travel. To the south, not too far away, was the border into Austria, but that country was also communist, and he knew he wouldn't fare any better there. To the north and west was the German border, where the Allied governments now occupied the land. Ironically, this area of so much danger and suffering in his recent past was now the direction he knew he should go. He would be safe, like others who had been forced to flee, if he could get there.[2]

---

2   There is another account of escape through the same route by Miloslav Rechcigl, Jr. in his memoir *Czechmate: From Bohemian Paradise to American Haven.*

So Father John began his journey. He started his motorcycle and rode to a home near Veseli, where he had planned to visit and bless a sick acquaintance anyway. Once this "excuse" for travel was over, however, Father John knew it would be too dangerous for him to ride further on the public roads. He abandoned his motorcycle and began to walk.

He traveled only on back, country roads and across private fields. To the north and west he walked, never really sure where he was, crossing meadows and marshes. He needed to avoid being seen completely, since there was no way to know who was an STB informant. He also knew that if someone helped him in any way that they would be placing their own lives at risk, and he did not want to endanger anyone.

After several hours of walking, Father John gradually began to feel the hunger, thirst, and tiredness that was so familiar to him during those three years in Grenzweg. It brought back horrible memories and visions in the dark. Now, more than ever before, he longed for freedom. He had had enough of life without it, and was just plain sick of it all.

He walked all through the night. As the sun rose on Good Friday morning, Christ's crucifixion day, Father John was relieved to at least know for sure which direction was east again. Back in Cerna that morning, the two STB informants were searching unsuccessfully all over town for the priest, in confusion and anger. They had no idea where he was, and in all honesty, neither did any of his parishioners.

Father John had nothing with him to eat. He found a place to hide and rest during the daylight hours of Good Friday. His weary legs and mind made it so easy to remember and meditate upon Christ's passion. Reaching into his coat pocket to get a cigarette, Father John felt the key to his church instead. He would later remember, "It was by accident because I hadn't planned to take the key with me." It was useless to him now, but it brought him a ray of joy, because it was comforting to have at least one "memento" from home.

As the day dragged on, and evening began to fall, Father John thought about all of the Catholic churches in the world that night which were open and bare, vigil lights extinguished, quietly reflecting the emptiness of the world after Christ's death. Father John prayed for his parishioners. Their church, too, was empty of the Eucharistic presence, and likely would remain that way for a long time.

The sunlight completely disappeared, and Father John was off again, walking north and west. It was difficult to navigate in the dark. Father John used his flashlight sparingly, knowing that soon he would reach the beginning of the Bohemian Forest which separated Germany and Czechoslovakia. In this dense forest he knew he would feel more safe but be less able to navigate. As he got closer to the edge of the forest there were more police guards patrolling. There were also barbed wire fences and minefields, built by the Germans during the war, that had not yet been cleared by the communist government. Providentially, Father John was able to avoid all of these dangers, and he made it safely into the protection of the mountainous forest right at the dawn of Holy Saturday.

Feeling hungry and exhausted, he picked out a hidden spot on dry ground and laid down to rest. He immediately fell into a deep sleep, but it was strewn with anxieties and nightmares. If you've ever spent the night on still partially-frozen ground, then you can imagine how stiff Father felt when he awoke several hours later. With only a cigarette for lunch, he knew he needed to hurry up and get going again. Hunger is a horrible feeling, and he was fleeing that hunger now as much as he was the Czech government.

Father John quickly became utterly lost in the steep, dense forest. Holy Saturday dragged on in overwhelming hunger, discomfort, and the fear that he was merely walking in circles. All he had to eat was snow. At one point while crossing an icy creek in the forest, he lost one of his shoes.

As the last rays of sunlight began to disappear that Holy Saturday night in the forest, Father tried to distract his thoughts of hunger and frustration. He began to think of the special liturgy that other priests were beginning to celebrate in Churches all around the world to commemorate Christ's Resurrection. It was during the darkness of that very first Easter morning that Christ rose victorious from the dead, conquering Satan and death for all eternity. Usually a deacon at each parish begins this liturgy by singing the ancient praise called the *Exsultet*. Father John tried to remember the words:

> *It is truly right that with full hearts and minds and voices*
> *we should praise the unseen God, the all-powerful Father,*
> *and his only Son, our Lord Jesus Christ.*
> *For Christ has ransomed us with his blood,*
> *and paid for us the price of Adam's sin to our eternal Father!*

Next, the hymn recalls the first Jewish Passover in Egypt when God saved his Chosen People from slavery. Each family had wiped the blood of an "unblemished" lamb on its door-posts so that the final, terrible plague would "pass over" their homes: the death of all first-born sons. When Pharaoh's own son died, he finally permitted the Jews to leave Egypt. God went before them "in a pillar of cloud by day and in a pillar of fire by night." (Num 14:14) Night is a grand symbol of death. The Easter Candle, which is lit and carried into the darkened Church during the liturgy, reminds parishioners that night is now and forever illuminated by the light which is Christ. The hymn declares:

> *This is our Passover feast,*
> *When Christ, the true Lamb, is slain,*
> *whose blood consecrates the homes of all believers.*
> *This is the night,*

> when first you saved our fathers:
> you freed the people of Israel from their slav'ry,
> and led them dry-shod through the sea.
> This is the night,
> when the pillar of fire destroyed the darkness of sin.
> This is night,
> when Christians ev'rywhere,
> washed clean of sin and freed from all defilement,
> are restored to grace and grow together in holiness.
> This is the night,
> when Jesus broke the chains of death
> and rose triumphant from the grave.

Father John now intimately understood the plight of the Israelites as they fled from Egypt, their home for 400 years, and entered the vast, barren desert. In order to be free they had to leave behind all things familiar, trusting in God's providence, and this was a most uncomfortable process. Father John knew that God gives us these dramatic stories in the Old Testament Scriptures to be symbols for each of our own lives. We all have a "desert" to navigate before we reach our true "Promised Land" in Heaven. Without the Resurrection, as the Exsultet continues, this journey would be meaningless:

What good would life have been to us,
had Christ not come as our Redeemer?
Father, how wonderful your care for us!
How boundless your merciful love!
To ransom a slave you gave away your Son.
O happy fault, O necessary sin of Adam,
which gained for us so great a Redeemer!

All evening long, with no idea where he was, Father John continued his way through the dark, hilly forest. Then unexpectedly, he heard a sound he hadn't heard in years… the ringing of Church bells. They were announcing the end of the long Easter Vigil Mass. Was he dreaming? No, Father John knew that he had made it to Germany because the bells were not allowed in Czechoslovakia. He was tired and hungry, but as he hurried on toward the sound, Father John felt the hand of God on his life, he felt the sweet joy of freedom, and he praised God for the gift of His Son.

Most blessed of all nights,
chosen by God to see Christ rising from the dead!
Of this night scripture says:
"The night will be as clear as day:
it will become my light, my joy."
The power of this holy night dispels all evil,

washes guilt away, restores lost innocence,

brings mourners joy;

it casts out hatred, brings us peace,

and humbles earthly pride.

Night truly blessed,

when heaven is wedded to earth

and we are reconciled to God!

"I was in the forest and I didn't know where I was. Then I began hearing the bells of a church ringing. I knew that couldn't be coming from any church in Czechoslovakia because of the communist crackdown on the churches. As I followed the sound of the bells I realized I had crossed the border into West Germany and I was safe."

When Father John finally came upon the Church with the bells he had heard, it was around midnight. He knocked on the door of the rectory and waited. After a few anxious minutes, someone cracked opened the door and said unmistakably, "Go away!" Father tried to explain himself, though he didn't speak hardly any German, but the man wouldn't listen. The door was quickly shut and locked in his face.

While reflecting on this incident decades later, Father John said: "I think that is the reason I have a different feeling for people who are in trouble, poor, and who are in need. I live on the highway here and every bum stops - I know some of them are just living from one church to another - but I cannot tell them 'no' when they come here and ask for help. I can see myself standing there. I would rather be laughed at than to turn away someone who needed help like I was that night when I needed help."

Heavily disappointed, but not deterred, Father John continued walking westward. He was confident that there had to be someone else nearby who would help him. He was right. The Allied armies who occupied Germany had set up numerous military camps, and many were close to the borders. Before long, Father John saw smoke rising in the distance and came upon a village, where he was welcomed in and allowed to spend the night in the local jail. He would later recall: "I didn't know the German language, I was alone in a strange city, without food, with only one shoe and I had no place to go, but I was so happy that I yelled myself hoarse. I was free."

The next morning, he was put on a train to Munich. After arriving, he recalled, "I then walked into town, looking for a church. When I knocked on the door of a monastery and asked for food, I was given two hamburgers - the best-tasting hamburgers of my life... Never in my life have I tasted anything so good." The brother at the monastery also gave him a few supplies.

The process for becoming a registered refugee involved staying at the military camp, filling out paperwork, and waiting to have your identity and background checked against Nazi participation. Father

John was not by far the only man in his position. Germany was in fact flooded with people fleeing communist persecution. Unfortunately, the living conditions at the camp were crowded and miserable. From the monastery, Father John walked back to the camp, recalling:

> And when I returned to camp with a razor, soap, towel, a spoon and five marks (about a dollar) that the brothers gave me, I was the richest man in camp. The men stood in line to use my spoon. The only forks or spoons in camp were those the men had fashioned from whatever was to be found in the trash pile…
>
> The food was terrible and everyone lived in squalor. Like myself, they had all escaped with only the clothes on their backs. Now they had to wait until a new home could be found for them and it often took a long time. But there was hope in the camp, because the people were free, and that's all that really mattered. Having lived without freedom, we all knew it was our most precious possession. This is something Americans cannot understand, because too many of them take this freedom for granted.

The rest of that Easter Sunday in the camp, Father John thought of little besides his family: "My family was expecting me home for Easter, and it was to be years before they would even know if I were alive." He missed his parents horribly. It took fourteen days for Father John's records to be checked, "and then I was told I was free to go where I chose… I had lost everything - my home, my family, my dreams - and my heart ached, but paradoxically I was ecstatically happy. *I was free.*"

A priest near Munich, in Oberndorf, upon learning that Father John was in the military camp, invited him to come stay at his rectory. It was now May of 1949. Father John happily accepted the offer, and for the next several months he stayed at the parish, assisted with the sacraments, and began learning conversational German.

Before long, Father John heard about a refugee camp in Ludwigsburg called Jagerhofkaserne. Hundreds of refugees were in the camp, including 220 Czech college students who had been forcibly exiled from their country. Though free to leave at any time, the students were mostly penniless, with little idea where to go next. A priest named Father Petr Levaky had been assigned to the camp as an Apostolic Delegate to assist the refugees, and he was in desperate need of more help. Father John knew immediately that he would like such a job, and with the blessing of his host, left Munich for Ludwigsburg.

Though he had plenty of work to do in the refugee camp and was grateful for the help he was receiving in Germany, Father John did not feel any need to stay in that country. He was free to go anywhere he wanted. There was one country continually in his imagination: the United States. Not only had the American soldiers liberated him from the labor camp and defeated the Nazis, but America was also generously shipping supplies to Germany to be donated to the refugees. He remembered, "As I handed out the coats and sweaters and mittens to those in need I began once more to envision a country so noble and kind as to care enough to share all that it had with those less fortunate - America."

As the weeks passed by, Father John met other Czech priests who had been forced to flee. He learned that six others had recently received passage to the United States and had been welcomed into the diocese of Lincoln, Nebraska. The bishop there, the Very Rev. Louis Kucera, happened to be Czech by nationality. In fact, there were entire parishes in Nebraska formed by Czech natives, where the Mass homilies were even preached in Czech. To Father John, this seemed to be a perfect arrangement. He sent off a letter of request to Bishop Kucera, who immediately replied and offered to begin the necessary arrangements.

First, all of the necessary resettlement documents were filled out in Lincoln, signed by the Bishop, and then sent to the American Consulate in Stuttgart, Germany. The forms were approved and the Consulate issued a visa for Father John to travel to America. An organization called the Catholic Committee for Refugees (CCR) in New York City then arranged and paid for all of the necessary transportation. At the same time that documents were prepared for Father John, they were also prepared for another refugee priest, Father

Vaclav Sladky, who also traveled to Nebraska and became a close friend of Father John's.

So after thirteen months in Germany, Father John set sail aboard the SS General Steward on May 30th, 1950, departing from Bremerhaven. Unlike most other passengers on the ship, who each had several large bags or trunks of luggage with them, he had only one small bag of supplies that had been given to him, plus his visa, his hat, and his long black coat. And still in the pocket of that coat was the only remembrance of his former life in his home country: a solitary key to the church in Cerna.

He arrived in New York on June 6th. A member of the CCR met him at the port and arranged for his train ride west. Bishop Kucera received a telegram stating that Father John would be stopping in Chicago to visit an acquaintance, and then would travel on to Lincoln.

As soon as Father John left Germany, Fr. Petr Levaky sent Bishop Kucera the following letter from Ludwigsburg:

> *...As far as Father Prachar was during several months until the last days of his stay in Germany my assistant in the religious administration of the Czechoslovakia refugee camp Jagerhofkaserne, Ludwigsburg, I testify that he was every time very zealous as far as his life and activity regards.*
>
> *I hope your Excellency will see very soon that you have helped a good priest. I should like to use this occasion to*

express my best thanks to your Excellency for all favours you are doing for our priests.

I remain in Christ very truly Yours,

Rev. Petr Levaky.

This is a letter written from Germany by Father John in 1950 to Bishop Kucera in Lincoln informing him of his departure date. Lincoln diocesan archives.

"I never had any regrets about the decision I made. I had two choices. One was to go to prison and live life without freedom... The second choice was to leave. I knew I could be useful someplace else." Bishop Kucera in Nebraska knew that he'd be useful, too.

In 1950 when Father John first stepped foot in Nebraska, there were already a dozen Czech parishes that had formed in the diocese, along with one German and two Polish-speaking parishes. Though he immediately began learning English, there was no shortage of Czech-speaking immigrants to welcome him and assist his transition to America. In fact, the earliest Czech priests arrived in Nebraska before there were any cars or paved roads, and would travel by foot, horseback, or wagon from Czech settlement to Czech settlement!

The Sacred Consistorial Congregation in Rome approved Father John's transfer of diocese for a period of three years. After that time, it was assumed that he'd be able to return home. Initially, Father John received residence at St. Clara's Home in Lincoln, a home for aging and sick priests, and was assigned to serve as a part-time assistant at Cathedral Parish while he became acclimated to the country and studied English.

The second place in the diocese where Bishop Kucera needed Father John was in the town of David City, where he served as an assistant in St. Mary's Parish and at St. Joseph's Villa, the first Catholic home for the aged in the diocese. Father John was the second priest to be named chaplain of the home. He served January 15th, 1951 until June 24th, 1951, when he was replaced by Father John Smutney, another priest who had recently arrived from Czechoslovakia. Father Smutney would become a life-long friend of Father John's.

The 1950's were an exciting, prosperous time to be in America, and Father John quickly fell in love with the good-hearted people he met everywhere in Nebraska. He loved the spaciousness of the country-sides, the charm of the small farming towns, the sunsets that stretched so wide along the western horizon that his eyes couldn't take all the glory of it in. Yet above all he cherished his freedom to fully live the vocation of a priest of God and preach to his heart's content without fear of reprisal.

Three years passed. Bishop Kucera requested an extension of the diocesan transfer from the Vatican, stating in the documents, "Father Prachar's work in the Lincoln [Diocese] has been most satisfactory. He is outstanding for his virtue, zeal for souls, and love for the Church." [August 24, 1954] Rome sent a three-year extension. Receiving the one-page document, complete with the seal of his Roman Pontiff, Father John could only sigh with sadness. In all this time, he still hadn't had any contact with his relatives back in Czechoslovakia. Would this be the first of many extensions? Time would prove it so.

Back home, the communist officials labeled Fr. John an "enemy of the people" and sentenced him to death should he be found. The end of the regime was no where in sight. In a much later newspaper interview, Father John said, "I thought my stay [in Nebraska] would be temporary, that the communist rule in Czechoslovakia would collapse, and I would be able to return. But that has not happened. My people would willingly die for their freedom, but they don't even have any guns. You don't fight tanks with sticks… Czechoslovakia will always be my true home, but I love it here."

Father continued to minister to the people. In 1953 he was appointed Vice Chairman of the St. Mary's High School building project, also in David City. Certainly it is no easy task to create a high school! The building committee raised $181,000 in one year. Father John was long remembered for his hard work helping to bring the school to fruition. In 1956, he became a deserving, naturalized US citizen.

This image was published by the Southern Nebraska Register on 8/10/56 announcing Father John's assignment to the parish of Bee. Lincoln diocesan archives.

Next, Father John was made pastor of St. Wenceslaus parish in the small town of Bee, where he served from 1956 through 1966. A memorable event during this decade was a trip he made to Europe in 1960, not to his beloved homeland, but to Germany. "I went to Germany to retrace my steps… I visited the parish near Munich where I was an assistant to the local pastor and to my surprise found the old pastor still there, the same housekeeper and my room - the same as it was when I left." He also visited the monastery where ten years earlier he had been given help and hamburgers, and Father John repaid them a hundredfold.

This photo is from the Omaha World Herald, June 30, 1974, to accompany an article by Andrea Doerr about Father John, which included a description of his 1960 trip to Germany where he re-paid the monastery which had given him hamburgers when he was starving. Photo copyright Omaha World Herald.

This image is dated 1/12/73 and was published in the Southern Nebraska Register with an article announcing that Father John had been awarded the Americanism Medal by the Daughters of the American Revolution. Lincoln diocesan archives.

Father John's subsequent assignments were to the towns of Brainard (1966-1968), Greenwood (June and July of 1969), and Saint Stephen's near Lawrence (1969-1973.) He became a 4th Degree Knight of Columbus. He liked to draw caricatures of himself, and he had artistic penmanship. In 1973, Father John again visited Europe. He spent six weeks there this time, and went to England, Germany, and Italy. In England he was able to meet up with a niece, later telling a reporter,

> I visited my niece in London. She was born after I left my home. She is the only member of my family living in the free world. She went through grade school, high school, and college under Communist rule, but left the country when the Russians invaded in 1968.

Through her, Father John was able to learn many details about his family and homeland. She was Father John's only relative living in a free country then.

In Germany, he visited the memorial of the Dachau concentration camp and, standing beside the ovens, prayed for the souls of friends who had died there. In Italy, he took part in a celebration marking the millennium anniversary of the founding of the first diocese in Czechoslovakia. The celebration was in Rome, and 400 Czech exiles from around the world had gathered together, including 35 priests. Father John was the only priest from the United States able to attend. He described an important part of the event:

> The main celebration was the special devotion in St. Peter's Basilica honoring St. Wenceslaus, the patron saint of Czechoslovakia. We went down into the crypt

to visit the grave of Cardinal Beran who had spent most of his life in prison, first in Dachau, and then on return to Czechoslovakia he was imprisoned again for 20 years and then exiled.

While in Italy, Father John had the privilege of a private audience with Pope Paul VI at his summer home, Castel Gandolfo. He would later rank it as a "top three" best event of his life!

This photo was published by the Southern Nebraska Register 11/2/73. It shows Pope Paul VI greeting Father John at a private audience at Castel Gandolfo, Italy. Image copyright Southern Nebraska Register.

On June 29th, 1973, Father John began an assignment as pastor of the parishes in Superior and Nelson. Here he baptized my younger brother and I as infants. In Superior he helped build and dedicate an outdoor Marian shrine, and as in each parish he served, was sure to erect a large flagpole outside the church, complete with floodlights for night time. He would explain, "I fly the flag in front of the Church both day and night because I know that as long as the flag flies, then I'm free."

In 1975, Father John was able to fly to London for his niece's wedding. His sister, the niece's mother, was given permission by the communist Czech government to attend the wedding and stay in London for a total of three weeks. It was the first time in 25 years that Father John and his sister had seen each other; it was an emotional and joyous reunion. The following year, Father John fulfilled a life-long dream of traveling to the Holy Land. Saying Mass on the Hill of Calvary was, he would later say, the most moving event of his life. He brought back the altar candles from that Mass and burned them the following Good Friday at the church in Superior.

One day Father found a stray brown terrier dog outside his rectory. He called the radio station to report the lost pet, but no one claimed him. So Father called back to the radio station and threatened that if the owner didn't show up, he would baptize the dog and then the town would have to contend with another Catholic in town! Father ended up keeping the dog and named him Bum.

By 1980, Father John had been serving Nebraskans for thirty years, had become a United States citizen, and had made America his home. In an interview in 1980, he said that even if he could return to Czechoslovakia, he wouldn't stay there for good. "This is where I'll rest my bones," he had decided. Father John had a knack for wrong predictions.

In 1981 Father John was given what would turn out to be his final assignment, as pastor of St. Catherine's parish in the town of Indianola. Father John was an extrovert who loved being around people and getting involved in the communities he lived in. In small towns, a common way to socialize is to attend the local high school sporting events, which Father John regularly did. Several Indianola parishioners recall seeing Father John at football games wearing a bright yellow DeKalb seed corn jacket and fur cap… that is, until the Bishop asked him to stop wearing such bright colors in public! Sometimes to accommodate sporting events father would change daily Mass times and joke that it was all in honor of "Saint Football." Attending games was a successful way of connecting with the youth of his parish.

Father was also remembered for calling other men "John" and the women "Mary," and before each baptism would pretend that these were the infant's names. Friends recall him constantly joking and telling stories. The diocese began administering "compatibility tests" to engaged couples in the diocese, and while Father John was in

Indianola, a couple he was preparing for marriage was the first couple to take one. They scored "highly compatible," and for years after their marriage, Father John would greet them with the joke, "so are you divorced yet?"

Father John brought his dog, Bum, to Indianola. He made a good companion and was just the excuse Father needed to go for frequent walks into town and visit with people. Father was a heavy smoker by the time he moved to Indianola. There's a story that one day he quit, cold turkey. Apparently he had been instructing a potential convert in the faith, and finally the man said he'd start coming to Mass if Father would quit smoking. So he did. The man was confirmed and sometimes would help bring the offering up during Mass, and would slip in a package of cigarettes in the basket to tempt Father! Yet he never smelled of smoke again.

Father John was understandably a very patriotic man who knew like few others the precious value of the term, "freedom." "It is almost impossible to define freedom," he said. "It is like trying to define love, and how can you explain love to someone who has never been in love? It's the same as trying to explain freedom to someone who has never lost it. You can only say what it isn't. And it isn't a concrete feeling." He offered his Christmas Eve Masses for the intentions and needs of all prisoners of war. He was presented the Americanism Medal by the National Society of the Daughters of the American Revolution.

He understood that in some situations around the globe, there are people, communities, even entire nations in need of rescue or support from the outside. He never tired of insisting that because America had been blessed with unparalleled prosperity, she should *want* to assist other nations around the globe who were in bondage.

"I say open your eyes, America! Wake up before it is too late! You have so much, you value it so little!"

"Granted, that life is not perfect in the United States. True, there are many areas that need correcting but at one and the same time people live better and complain more in the United States than anywhere else in the world. Let us take just one area of life - taxes. Taxes are high, but they are the cheapest rent one can pay for living free. Any doubters should live under the prison of the red [communist] regime for one month and there would be no more complaints from anyone."

"If I didn't love the United States, or if I felt we were secure from communism, I wouldn't go out to speak. But I know that the most effective weapon against communism is informed citizens... The greatest danger to the U.S. is disinterest on the part of its citizens."

Whenever invited, he would give so-called "freedom speeches" and interviews, adding:

> Please don't make me sound like a hero. I do not wish
> to be made some sort of celebrity. My sole purpose in
> talking with others about my life and the true value of

our great democracy is to ensure that in time to come little kids running free today won't have to stand in complete subjection as adults, thinking about how wonderful life used to be.

Earlier, during the Vietnam War, Father John developed strongly negative opinions about "dodging" the military service draft. "I don't want to get into politics. Whatever I say is my opinion, not that of my church, neither do I want to condemn any church leaders who have been involved [in the anti-Vietnam-war movement]."

At the same time, he was also quite vocal about the importance of ecumenism in the goal of furthering world peace. For too much of his life, he had witnessed discrimination based on ethnic and religious differences. He came to believe that preventing such bias and discrimination begins by focusing on common ground and learning to love people of other Christian denominations. He befriended many protestant ministers in the towns where he lived, and hoped that this would set an example or his parishioners to live peaceably with their fellow Americans. He said:

> The ecumenical movement is the first step in the right direction [towards global peace]… we must learn to respect each other and work together as brothers and sisters… When we think of the things which divide us and then start thinking of the things which unite us we

will find there are more things on which we agree than on which we disagree. Our prejudices have built up over the centuries and they won't go away over night. We must keep working at it…

This is a Christian nation and in our unity we can defeat any enemy. I'm sure trying to promote that unity. It is my way of saying thanks for my freedom… It is beautiful to be free. America is free. America is beautiful.

308-364-2428

Father John Prachar

An Intelligent, Caring, Handsome,
Wonderful, Patient, Loving,
Eloquent, Jovial,
and HUMBLE priest

P.O. Box 10
Indianola, NE

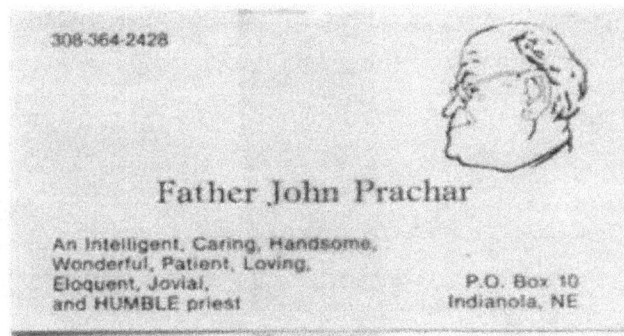

Father John's business card.

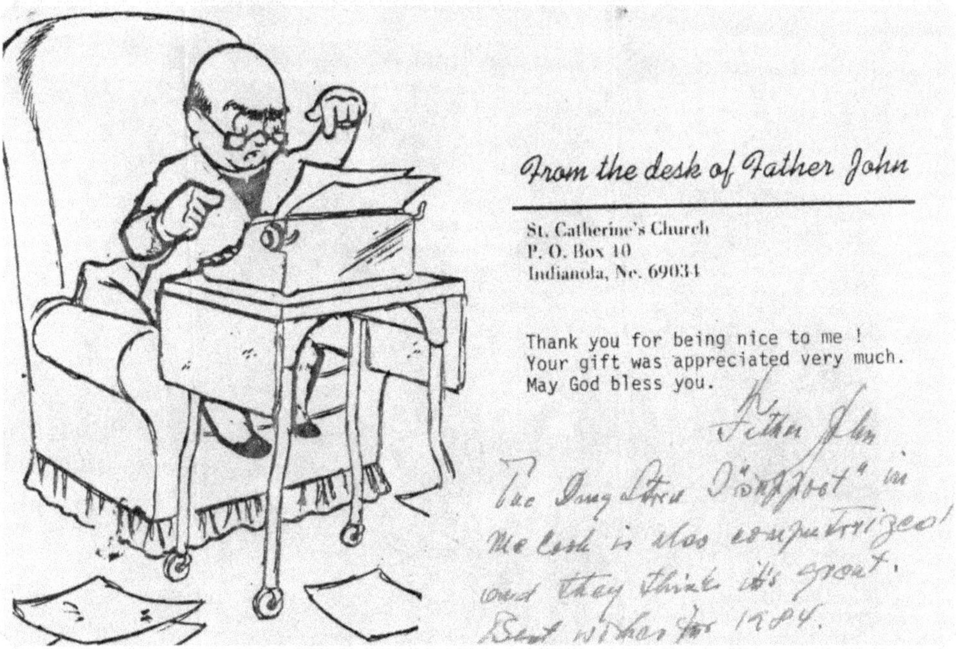

From the desk of Father John

St. Catherine's Church
P. O. Box 10
Indianola, Ne. 69034

Thank you for being nice to me !
Your gift was appreciated very much.
May God bless you.

Father John

and they think it's great.
Best wishes for 1984.

This is a thank-you note sent by Father John in 1984.

This image of Father John accompanied an article written by Father Kenneth Borowiak in the Southern Nebraska Register on September 1st, 1989.

By 1985, Father John had lived for 35 years in America. That year, he made contact with some friends back home in Czechoslovakia; they then visited the town of Cerna and took a picture of the church and sent it to Father, who framed it and hung it in his office. They told him that the front door of the church had never been opened since he had locked it so long before. Also in Father John's office in Indianola was the key to that front door, which he had galvanized. It was the only remnant of his homeland, and as such was a precious memento. Father said in an interview, "I kept it all these years, in the hope that someday I could go back and return the key to it's rightful place."

Four years later, in November of 1989, a miracle occurred. The Communist government in Czechoslovakia was finally defeated, without a single gunshot being fired, in what was called the Velvet (or Silk) Revolution. As a Christmas gift from his parishioners the following month, Father John received with tears a round-trip plane ticket from Omaha, Nebraska, to Prague. "Did you ever pray for anything that you knew was never going to happen, but you kept on praying for it anyway? Well that is exactly what I did, I prayed every day for forty years about going back. And it finally happened."

This image was published in the McCook Gazette in early 1990. It accompanied an article about Father John by Robert Pore. Image copyright the McCook Daily Gazette.

His visa was granted, and Father John boarded his flight, filled head-to-toe with excitement. Stepping foot back in his homeland was an indescribable joy. He recalled, "To see them free, it [was] beautiful!" He visited family and friends, including two sisters, and he saw the graves of his parents. Though Father was thrilled about his journey, there was also one sad event that happened. His brother, Frank, had recently had surgery for cancer, but his health deteriorated quickly and he died while Father John was visiting. Father said the funeral Mass. Ironically, the last Mass Father had said in that particular church had been Frank's wedding Mass.

Father's nephew, Vaclav, drove him south to the town of Cerna. Locals asked him if he intended to move back for good. "I made it very clear that my heart was with them but my home was in Indianola." When he got to the church, as he recalled, "I put the key in the door, turned it, and it opened. It fit!" Local parishioners asked him to keep the key as a memento and return the following year for another visit, which he certainly intended to do.

This photo was published 3/12/90 in the Lincoln Journal Star, on page 8. It accompanied an AP wire story about Father John from Indianola. Image copyright AP wire service.

****

June, 1991. Father John was aboard a flight to Vienna, Austria, and safely packed in his bag was his return ticket to Omaha. Tragically, that return flight would not include him.

The parishioners in Nebraska later received this letter of explanation from Vaclav Penka, Father John's nephew[3]. He wrote:

> My uncle was expected to come to Prague from Vienna on June 6th. My mother and I were waiting at the airport, but uncle didn't arrive. Later that day he rang [phoned] us from a hotel in Vienna, saying he had been mugged and robbed, and was asking me to come to Vienna to pick him up. The hotel manager informed me they had to call a doctor due to his medical condition. I left for Vienna that night.
>
> When I found the hotel where he stayed, the management told me he was in the hospital. I found the hospital and spoke to my uncle as well as his doctors. It was decided then, that he should stay on at

---
3 The letter was translated and penned by Vaclav's sister, who was visiting from London, and who was much more fluent in English than he. For the sake of readability, I have made some insignificant grammar changes.

the Vienna hospital due to his condition. After four days I received a call from that same hospital, to come and pick my uncle up, that he is now well. It was June 10th now, and I was going back to Vienna to bring him home to Cernovice.

He was with us for about a week during which time he met some of his friends and relatives, but didn't want to go anywhere due to his [new] medical problems. [Incontinence, soreness, tiredness.] I took him to a hospital in Pelhremov, where he received good medical care and had felt better again. However before the end of the week we noticed that he was having breathing problems. Even though he was reassuring us all was well, we called emergency help, who took him at once to the hospital. This happened on Sunday, June 17th.

The same night, I went to see him in the hospital, and found my uncle sitting on the bed saying, "let's go home. I feel better." However the surgeon in charge informed me that in the attack uncle received three broken ribs which were pressing into one side of his lungs and due to this, that side of his lungs were ceasing to function. The next day we were informed that his condition had deteriorated and he had to be transferred into the intensive care unit, where he was put onto a life support machine. He was receiving the best medical care possible (at all times) and I was informed daily of his condition.

Friday, June 28th, his condition improved to the extent that my parents and I could visit him. We were all very happy that he was improving and that we would be able to make his stay in Czechoslovakia pleasant again. But on Sunday morning, June 30th, we were told by his doctors that his condition had deteriorated once more and was quite critical due to his long running diabetes and heart condition. At about 10 a.m. that same morning we were informed that he had passed away. He did receive the Holy Sacrament of Anointing from the local priest before he died. It was a deep shock for all of us.

Now the case is in the hands of INTERPOL, as well as all of us trying to find out what really happened, since my uncle didn't want to talk about it when I asked him. The US Embassy in Vienna was informed by my uncle that he had fallen down the stairs. It is very difficult to find out what happened, and it looks as if the investigation is going to take some time…

This week on Tuesday, August 13th, I returned the gold plated church key to the parishioners at Cerna in Posumava, which used to be my uncle's parish. We are all extremely sad at the way our meeting turned out. All we have now are memories and are trying to come to terms with it all. I have lots of lovely memories from our meetings. I shall write again.

Vaclav Penka

PS. Lots of love and greetings from my parents and my two sisters.

The signature of Vaclav Penka when he wrote to the people of Nebraska to explain the death of his uncle. I have been unsuccessful in my attempts to contact Vaclav and the relatives of Father John.

Father John was buried following a funeral Mass at 2:00 p.m. on Wednesday, July 10th, 1991, in the cemetery of Choustnik, the same town where he had been baptized, near the graves of his parents.

Certainly the news of Father John's death was a shock to

everyone who knew him in Nebraska. On Tuesday, July 9th, at 11:00 a.m., a Memorial Mass was held for Father John in the small town of Indianola, presided over by Bishop Glennon P. Flavin and attended by more than 500 people, as the flag outside the church flew at half-mast. During his homily, Bishop Flavin said, "He was a happy man and a holy man. He was devoted to the people of his parish and to others. Once in a lifetime do you meet a man like Father John. We will all miss him."

The circumstances of his death would always remain a mystery.

This photo was published on the front page of the McCook Daily Gazette on 7/10/91 showing the funeral Mass of Father John inside St. Catherine's Catholic Church in Indianola. Image copyright the McCook Daily Gazette.

*Bůh je láska, kdo zůstává v lásce,
zůstává v Bohu, a Bůh zůstává v něm.*
1. Jan 4, 16

Příbuzným, známým, kněžím a věřícím oznamujeme,
že Bůh k Sobě povolal svého věrného služebníka

Very Reverend

JANA PRACHAŘE

kněze v St. Catherines kostele, Indianola, Nebraska — USA

Narodil se 8. dubna 1918 v Dlouhé Lhotě.
Na kněze byl vysvěcen v roce 1946 v Českých Budějovicích.
Působil ve Veselí nad Lužnicí a v Černé v Pošumaví.
Od roku 1949 působil v různých farnostech v USA.

Zemřel při návštěvě vlasti, v pelhřimovské nemocnici,
v neděli dne 30. června 1991, na následky zranění.
Zemřel posilněn svátostí nemocných.

Se zemřelým se rozloučíme ve středu dne 10. července 1991
o 14. hodině ve farním kostele v Choustníku.
Po mši svaté uložíme zesnulého na místním hřbitově, kde bude
očekávat vzkříšení.

O modlitbu za zesnulého prosí:

Marie Janů a Anna Pěnková,   Farníci z Indianoly
sestry s rodinami   Spolubratří kněží
a ostatní příbuzní

Za projev soustrasti předem děkujeme.
V Černovicích, nám. Míru 89, dne 4. července 1991.

This is a copy of the funeral announcement for Father John sent to Nebraska by his sisters Marie Janu and Anna Penka.

Eternal rest grant unto him, O Lord,
and let perpetual light shine upon him.
May all the souls of the faithful departed rest in peace.
Amen.

Afterward

There is an on-line book about Czech churches in Nebraska here: http://www.unl.edu/Czechheritage/churches.pdf edited by Vladimir Kucera in 1974.

For more information about the treatment of Catholic clergy by the Nazi regime, I recommend the following books:

You Shall Be My Witnesses, Lessons Beyond Dachau, by Archbishop Kazimierz Majdanski.

Christ in Dachau, by Johann Maria Lenz

The Shadow of His Wings, the True Story of Fr. Gereon Goldmann, OFM, translated by Benedict Leutenegger

Priestblock 25487, A Memoir of Dachau, by Father Jean Bernard (This was adapted into the film *The Ninth Day*, but the book is very different from the movie.) Here is an excerpt:

> "...Since all the other members of the crew were Polish, the capo sometimes started a conversation with me during work, and I seized the opportunity to catch my breath without risking punishment. In these talks we spoke only about religion and religious matters. Sometimes the guards chimed in, too. At the end of them my adversaries always had the last word: "It's all nonsense and lies! And now get back to work!"

Once I had a guard who had obviously received some education, and I managed to get the better of him completely. I explained to him how, if God has created man with free will, He has to leave a back door open for unbelief despite all His revelations of Himself. For if He showed Himself to us too clearly, He would force us to believe and thus, having given us freedom with one hand, take it away with the other.

Another time I did something most unwise. After we had spoken for a whole morning about religious matters, the capo said, "I'm not changing my mind - I still don't believe in God!" Unable to resist the temptation, I responded, "Why do you talk about Him so much then?"

That put an abrupt end to our theological conversations..."

Author's Notes

Do you have any personal memories or photographs of Father John you would like to share? You can send me a message at:

FatherJohnsStory@gmail.com

Or visit the website:

FatherJohnsStory.com

Would you like to make a donation in memory of Father John? Consider one of the parishes he served or the UNL Czech Heritage Project: http://www.unl.edu/Czechheritage/

www.ingramcontent.com/pod-product-compliance
Lightning Source LLC
Chambersburg PA
CBHW071319040426
42444CB00009B/2052